THE APPRECIATIVE FACILITATOR

A HANDBOOK FOR FACILITATORS AND TEACHERS

Cheri B. Torres, MBA, MA

Copyright © 2001 by Cheri B. Torres
ISBN 0-9714416-0-X

Mobile Team Challenge
3247 E. Lamar Alexander Parkway
Maryville, TN 37804
(865)681-0146 fax (865)982-7721
Printed in the United States of America

This book is dedicated
to all those working to create
beauty, joy, peace, and abundance
on this planet.

THE PROMISE

This book is about seeing the world through different lenses. Becoming an appreciative facilitator or teacher means a commitment to change your life. The good news is that like your clients and students, you too will hold positive active images of the future for yourself and for others. Your world will become one filled with joy, beauty, hope, creativity, and the sparkle of personal motivation. This promises to have a most positive and profound effect on you!

TABLE OF CONTENTS

ACKNOWLEDGEMENTS

My sincere appreciation and gratitude goes to the people who made this book possible.

My thanks to David Cooperrider and Diana Whitney for introducing me to Appreciative Inquiry, and to my business partner, Carolyn "Rainey" Morton, for traveling with me on our journey to integrate the principles of Appreciative Inquiry into our facilitator training and our organization.

A special thanks to my husband, Michael for encouragement and help with editing, my daughters, Laura and Carmen, for supporting my work, my colleagues, Rainey and Monica Alsup, for their input and feedback, and for my mother, Bobbie Bogert, who helped with the editing and has provided life-long encouragement for me.

I would also like to acknowledge Simon Priest for his initial encouragement to write this book, and Sam Sikes for his support in getting the book published. And my special and sincere gratitude to the hundreds of Mobile Team Challenge members-- teachers and trainers--who have given us feedback on our Appreciative Facilitator Training.

INTRODUCTION

There is a growing realization among professionals from diverse disciplines that each of us plays a significant role in creating the reality in which we live, work, and play. Our beliefs, our attitude, where we place our attention, our thoughts, and the language we use determine in large part the images that we carry in our mind's eye. . . and these images are compelling.

Think about something you have created, built, or developed. Did you have an image of the project before you began, at least to some extent? The more detailed and descriptive your pre-plan, the greater the likelihood that it evolved to look just like that image. The image precedes everything.

We have all heard of placebos, those little inert or sugar pills that have no inherent medicinal value yet seem to "cure" patients. This Placebo Effect has been and continues to be investigated. Research suggests that the patient's belief in the medicine and the doctor as well as the images they carry related to their illness and health play an integral role in their healing process; for some, the leading role [*Appendix I*].

Time and time again doctors witness patient's recovery from diverse illnesses as the result of taking an inert pill, which the patient believes will cure them. In the field of medicine, additional research on the use of imagery is underscoring its vital role in the health and wellness of individuals. Studies at the University of California at Los Angeles (UCLA) have shown that simple imagery and visualization techniques can increase the number of B and T cells in our immune system, making it stronger and more efficient. A stunning example of imagery in healing is a patient who had an incurable heart condition known as a "Galloping Heart." The heart races out of control, and physicians are not able to stop it; it literally "beats itself to death" within 48 hours. A particular patient in a teaching hospital, however, did not know the name of his heart condition. When medical students made rounds with an unfamiliar physician, the physician simply named his condition, "This patient has a galloping heart," and read the patient's chart to the students. The group left the room, and the patient was left with his own image of what those words meant. Weeks later, after he had returned home completely cured, he was asked if he knew the turning point in his recovery. He replied, "When I heard I had a galloping heart all I could think of was a strong stallion, wild and free in the open. I just knew that meant that I was going to be able to lick whatever I had."

The power of imagery has been shown in a variety of other fields. In the field of education, research has documented the Pygmalion Effect [*Appendix I*], "As the teacher believes the student to be, so the student becomes." The beliefs the teacher holds are conveyed to the child through all forms of communication and her or his beliefs carry an energy all their own. The child reflects back those beliefs. Studies done where elementary school teachers were given random histories of academic and behavioral performance on their students showed that by the end of a school term students were performing according to the random histories rather than how they had actually performed prior to the study. The beliefs and images the teachers held were so powerful that they over-rode the children's own abilities and tendencies.

Witness the effect language and thoughts have upon your own state of mind and physiology as you respond to these two directives. *Recall the last time you "messed up." A time when you did a poor job on something or spoke when it would have been better to have been silent.* Hold the image in your mind and recall how you felt. Pause a moment. What do you notice about your energy level and sense of well being? Did you have an adrenaline or other hormonal response? What posture did your body assume? In what direction did your eyes turn? What expression came upon your face? What mood arose?

Now, *recall the last time you excelled at something important to you. You may have received positive feedback from others about your performance or people may have received great value from something you did.* Hold the image in your mind and recall how you felt. Pause a moment. What do you notice about your energy level and sense of well being? Did you have an adrenaline or other hormonal response? What posture did your body assume? In what direction did your eyes turn? What expression came upon your face? What mood arose?

These two simple questions lead the mind, body, emotions, and spirit in two totally different directions. Your thoughts and images release different hormones and neurotransmitters in the body, which effect the immune system, mood, temperament, and physical strength. They also effect posture, breath, and connection with the world around you. Now reflect on the kinds of conversations you have on a regular basis in your life, not to mention the silent conversations you carry on non-stop inside your own head. The questions we ask, the focus of our attention and our language has an immediate effect upon us and those around us.

Where we place our attention *does* impact the entire quality of our lives.

We are so compelled to move in the direction of the images that we carry that many athletes now train using visualization. It is not a substitute for actual practice, but combined with practice, athletes improve significantly more than just practice alone. Positive, successful images are vital. This was documented in one research effort where 50 individuals were taken to a controlled environment and taught to bowl [*ref.* D. Cooperrider]. At night half the group was shown video clips of all their mistakes and told to correct these mistakes. The other half of the group was shown video clips of all their successes and told to do more of what they saw. At the end of a week, all individuals had improved, but the half who had only viewed their successes was more than 100% better than the other group.

Repeatedly, data supports the idea that we must be vigilant about the images we carry in our heads, the images we expose ourselves to over and over, and the images we are creating for others in our lives. If you are a facilitator, educator, or trainer, the work you do continuously creates images and mindsets for those with whom you work. What beliefs and images do you hold about your clients or students? What language do you use? What questions do you ask and where do those questions lead your participants? For teachers and educational facilitators, these questions are further underscored by current research on learning. Brain-based education and facilitation requires us to pay attention to such detail.

This book is about conscious teaching and facilitation—not just being a good facilitator/teacher, but also being an *appreciative* facilitator/teacher. This means choosing words that support positive images for clients or students. It means carefully crafting questions that support positive reflection and action. And it means having the tools and techniques available to support profound positive images that lead your clients and students to actualize the wonderful things they learn while working with you. This book is also about facilitating experiential learning activities to develop core competencies using the appreciative perspective.

Chapter one paints a picture of the Appreciative Facilitator–what makes her or him unique and what you can do to develop your own appreciative skills and perspective.

Chapter two provides an overview of brain-based learning and presents the experiential learning process, methodology, techniques necessary for effective appreciative facilitation of activities.

Because crafting questions is so much a part of facilitating learning, Chapter three explores appreciative facilitation from the perspective of the question.

For those interested in the specifics of the "pure" Appreciative Inquiry (AI) process, Chapter four provides a brief overview of AI and the AI Process. The end of this chapter summarizes the key principles of AI and underscores their impact on facilitation. Chapter five follows with a method for incorporating the AI process into experiential learning on a ropes course.

The appendices provide references, detailed outlines for experiential learning, resources for further reading, and websites for additional information about Appreciative Inquiry, experiential learning, and brain-based learning.

The appreciative paradigm is a rapidly spreading perspective in the world. It may be referred to by words other than "appreciative", but the concept will be the same. Mobile Team Challenge, the company I co-founded with Carolyn Rainey Morton in 1996, has incorporated AI into all that we do. Our belief is that each of us is a powerful change agent in our own life and in the lives of others. Our mission is to work together with people from around the world in order to influence positive change on our planet. We invite you to join us, and we welcome your feedback, input, and experiences as you use this approach to facilitate. You can contact us by phone at 888-681-0146 or email us at info@mobileteamchallenge.com.

Enjoy your reading and enjoy creating positive actions in your life and in the lives of others!

Chapter One

THE APPRECIATIVE FACILITATOR

What makes appreciative facilitators unique is their overall paradigm or world-view. This paradigm includes not only how they view the world, but also their beliefs about it. It colors their ideas, their language, and their focus of attention. They look at the world and the people in it *appreciatively*.

To appreciate is to see the value in something, to find the good and the worth. So the appreciative facilitator working with groups of people will look for what is of value, what is worthy, and what is good. They will explore whatever is going on from this vantage-point; it is almost as if they have flipped the problem-solving coin to the other side and asked, what are the solutions (already in existence and the potential)? They are not to be mistaken for "space cadets looking at the world through rose-colored glasses." Appreciative facilitators do not turn away from problems and challenges; but after acknowledging the situation and the people, they turn the conversation towards resolution.

You will recognize appreciative facilitators by the language they use. You will hear carefully chosen words that enrich, enliven, enthuse, and inspire the people they work with. You will hear language that affirms, acknowledges, and encourages. The language will lead listeners to envision positive images that are bold, grounded in both reality and dreams, and inspire listeners to move into those images.

If you explore the belief system of appreciative facilitators you will discover that their beliefs reflect the world as a place of possibility filled with competent, capable people who are eager to achieve the good. They will recognize that obstacles arise along the way, but these apparent problems are simply challenges to be met, opportunities in disguise.

Their belief in people's inherent desire to be effective and to do well comes through to their clients. People respond to the appreciative facilitator's belief in them, and it effects their own sense of what they can accomplish. The appreciative facilitator's beliefs may not be stated explicitly, but you will recognize their beliefs by the way they treat people in general. Their body and verbal language will reflect their respect and their assumptions about the abilities of others.

BEGIN WITH YOU – YOUR PRACTICES AND YOUR BELIEFS

Skilled Facilitation

Facilitation is the art of opening doors and windows for others. The skilled facilitator doesn't do the work, the group does. The skilled facilitator has no ego involved in the process. He or she simply supports awareness and insights, guiding others toward their desired outcome, and leaving them feeling they did it themselves. Skilled experiential facilitators create situations where learning opportunities abound; they use the Socratic method in ways that allow others to discover their own truths and abilities, taking no credit for the achievements.

The Appreciative Philosophy

The appreciative philosophy begins with acknowledging that each of us has some experience of a positive core, of working or being exceptional. We know how to do this, we just need to bring it to consciousness. Each of us has dreams and visions about the "best," the "ideal" and these are often based upon our moments of being at our best and seeing others at their best. We are all capable of changing, learning, growing, and achieving our dreams. We deserve to bring our best into play, we deserve to express the beautiful, and to be fully alive.

The Appreciative Facilitator

The appreciative facilitator practices skilled facilitation, is determined by the appreciative philosophy, and holds beliefs that are congruent. The appreciative facilitator pays conscientious attention to language and focus, eliminating deficit language and the "to be fixed" perspective. The appreciative facilitator reframes challenges or problems so they can be resolved in the context of best practices and future goals.

Becoming an appreciative facilitator is a process of changing habits. Even if we adopt a new awareness and intellectually decide to change our beliefs, we still have to work on old habits, which can be deeply ingrained. Staying conscious is the most challenging part. Be patient and compassionate with yourself if you find yourself falling into old habits. It's like meditating—when your mind wanders and you notice it, you simply bring your awareness back to where you want it. This is all about shifting out of cruise control and into personal control over behavior, language, and focus.

The first step in developing your skills as an appreciative facilitator is to examine your own beliefs. The following worksheet will help you do this.

What are your beliefs about your skills and abilities to empathize (tune into what others are feeling, their motives, perspectives, needs, etc.)? How do you achieve this?

_____

_____

_____

_____

_____

_____

Are you willing to take in cues and clues, withholding judgement? And what will that mean? What will you have to do to accomplish this?

_____

_____

_____

_____

_____

_____

Are you willing to question the cues and clues you currently look for; are you willing to examine your focus of attention closely?

_____

_____

_____

What would it mean to look for cues and clues that targeted a positive read on everyone?

_____

_____

_____

_____

_____

_____

What would it mean to reframe "negative" or "problem" behavior in such a way that it helped you become aware of an individual's unmet needs or fears?

_____

_____

_____

_____

_____

_____

_____

For you to believe in the inherent ability and goodness of people, what other beliefs or values would you have to change? *(One approach to unearthing this is to make the statement, "I believe that people are capable and good—the next time I have a group, I will act accordingly." Then listen for the inner dialogue that comes up. These are all the thoughts and beliefs that run counter to your statement. For example, you say, "I (your name)___, believe that people are basically good and competent" and the little voice inside your head says, "except for ____!" Keep repeating the affirmation and noticing the responses that you get until you have a complete understanding of all the beliefs you hold that limit your ability to think appreciatively of all people.)*

_____

_____

_____

_____

_____

_____

Recall a time when you facilitated a group that was competent, capable, in fact, they excelled. Reflect back on your beliefs about them, the language you used, how you carried your body, your facial expressions, tone of voice. How did you convey to them that you thought they were exceptional? What did you value about yourself as a facilitator with this client or group of students? What did you value about the client/students?

_____

_____

_____

_____

_____

_____

_____

_____

_____

_____

Can you entertain the idea that the only significant difference between the above group and a group you judge to be incompetent is either individual or collective fear, individual or collective lack of self-confidence/self-worth, or individual or collective lack of knowledge, skill, or understanding, rather than inherent incompetence?

_____

Your Commitment
In examining your belief system, it is imperative that you determine whether you are interested in making the necessary changes as well as willing to commit and be resolved to change your paradigm. The Pygmalion Effect is so powerful that regardless of what you intellectually decide to do, your beliefs will come through. Your beliefs carry their own energy and that impacts others.

To gradually shift your belief system, begin by deciding to simply suspend your beliefs about people. Stay open to the outcome. This is a challenge in and of itself, but very informative. Staying open means no judgements, no stereotyping, no preconceived notions. When you become aware that judgement is sneaking in, just remind yourself that you have chosen to stay open (never at the risk of safety, of course). When you find yourself noticing the negative, take responsibility for where you are choosing to place your attention, what thoughts you are allowing to dominate. Choose a different focus of attention.

Gradually, over time, if you stay open to people and focus on the positive, your belief system will begin to shift because of the shift in data that you are gathering about people and because of the new habit that you are forming. This does not mean that every action that people take will be positive or beneficial. It does not mean that bad things will not happen as the result of people's actions. It is merely a statement about beliefs regarding people's inherent being.

WHERE DO YOU FOCUS YOUR ATTENTION?

The next time you are at a mall, try this activity. *Walk to several shop windows and observe items for a minute at each window (choose windows that have lots of items in them). Then turn away and write down everything that you recall. Now, return to the windows, this time look for all the blue objects. Did you see anything you didn't see the first time? Then, come back and this time look for all the yellow objects. Again, did you see objects you didn't see the other two times?*

The point is, we see what we look for. The world is an open book and to a large extent, we are the creative artists. What we look for, see, and how we respond to it is the world we create for ourselves. . . and for others. When you work with others, you have specific outcomes in mind. Clients hire you with specific goals in mind, students show up with the hope of learning something that you have to teach. Look for examples and behaviors that correspond with where the client wants to go, times when they are achieving these goals, and look for success amongst the students. Ask questions that bring your audience's attention to these successes and help them develop those images into bold, dramatic images. Support their ability to create anchors to those images and specific visions of how this same kind of effective interaction will take place in another setting (work, school, or home).

For example, if the desired outcome is effective communication, then look for times when individuals communicate effectively. Invite them to recall these times in great detail. What was happening? What were their thoughts and feelings? What did they value about themselves and the others during the situation? What was the overall result of such quality communication? What supported their ability to communicate in this way? What would it be like to communicate in this way in the office or classroom? With such questions, you are able to fix the client's attention on success; you help the clients develop images that are anchors, which means they are more likely to communicate like this again in another situation.

Words Are Physical

Maya Angelou talks about the power of words. At an early age, realizing how powerful her own words were, she stopped talking for six years (*I Know Why the Caged Bird Sings*). To this day she is very careful about what kinds of words she will allow inside her home.

Words are one of the most powerful tools a facilitator or teacher uses. Thinking of words as actual physical, energetic entities may help you to take seriously the impact that they have upon you and others. As a facilitator, you guide the group. The questions you ask, the language you use will immediately lead the group in a specific direction. There are no neutral questions; there are no objective questions. The appreciative facilitator is conscious in carefully crafting questions and choosing words that will support the goals of the client or student.

If you believe in the individual, then the words that flow will reflect that. If you are focusing on the positive, then the words will flow from that source as well. If you are looking to shift attention from what is not working to what is working and what can work, then words will flow that support such forward movement. If you find yourself using habitual non-appreciative language or problem-oriented focusing, simply take a moment to reflect on what is driving your language. Is it preconceptions about the client? Has the language of the client or students determined your focus of attention? If you find yourself walking down a habitual path, simply ask an appreciative question. The energy, focus, and direction will immediately change.

If you Choose to Go Down this Path
When you decide to become an appreciative facilitator, be patient with yourself and enlist the support of at least one other colleague who also is interested in exploring appreciative facilitation. Support one another's new habit, gently nudging one another when old habits surface. Refrain from judging and comparing, simply redirect yourself when you become aware, redirect your colleague, and don't forget to use humor. Changing a habit can be a challenge, especially if the old habit has brought

rewards, affirmation, and accolades (how many of us have been praised for our problem-solving abilities!). The good news is that you can still "solve problems," you are simply using a different technique. Even better news, this technique promises to be faster, more direct, and create a great deal more joy, aliveness, and motivation along the way.

Chapter Two

EXPERIENTIAL LEARNING: THE WAY THE BRAIN LEARNS BEST

Learning involves (a) intake and comprehension of new data, (b) storage of that data, (c) retrieval of the data when needed, and (d) appropriate use of the data. Researchers have discovered that the whole human organism is involved in these activities, not just the brain. This book is not a text on brain-based learning (see resources for more information); however, a brief overview will enable you to fully appreciate the value of experiential learning and appreciative facilitation as it relates to facilitating/teaching, regardless of whether you are a teacher in a classroom or a trainer/consultant in the corporate world. We will then turn to focus specifically on experiential learning activities (primarily a low ropes course) to teach core competencies, life skills, and effective teamwork.

How the Brain Learns
Technological advancements have enabled researchers to literally see how the brain learns best. The process is complex, but the necessary components for effective learning are easily

summarized: *context, experience,* and *security/safety*
[S. Kovalik, C. Hannaford].

Context

The brain is an "associative organ"; it learns by
relating new data to current, stored information.
Thus, context is important. If new information is
presented in relationship to something known, the
brain has an effective way to "file" the data so that it
is more readily retrievable. Without a context, the
brain may file the data incorrectly or randomly,
making it difficult to retrieve or use appropriately.

Experience

Learning is a "whole person", neuro-physiological
process [Kovalik, Hannaford, Hart, Healy,
Schlechty]. It involves mind, body, and emotions. If
any one of these essential aspects is missing, the
learning process is impeded. The greater the sensory
involvement, the greater the learning potential. In
fact, if teaching strategies involve only listening (our
standard classroom, desk-style learning), the brain
retains just 10% of what it takes in; however, when
experiential opportunities are integrated so that the
whole person is involved--physically, mentally, and
emotionally--the brain retains more than 80% of what
it learns [Piaget, S. Kovalik]. Experiential learning
activities not only provide opportunities for the whole
person to be involved in the lesson, but they also

provide a context when combined with guided reflection, an essential component for effective learning.

Security/Safety

The brain is not the only organ involved in the learning process. The other key organ is the heart. Research documents that if a person feels threatened, fearful, intimidated, or rejected in some way, the brain actually "down shifts" [S. Randall]. The body/mind connection is nowhere more apparent than when we are emotionally threatened. The limbic system (the "seat" of our emotions) is directly connected to the heart; and the limbic system is a primary traffic control center in the brain. When the individual is threatened, a neural message is sent to the limbic system, which goes on alert. Attention is channeled to the R-complex in preparation for "fight or flight." The primary learning center in the brain (neo-cortex) "is by-passed" [L. Hart]; it never receives the incoming messages.

For effective learning then, the teacher/facilitator must establish an environment where individuals feel secure physically, emotionally, and mentally. The appreciative facilitator is a natural at this, using language that creates positive images and holding beliefs that convey support and honor for each person's inherent ability.

High Impact Learning
The three primary components for high impact learning are full-sensory relevant experience, security/safety, and context. For the facilitator/teacher, the challenge is in setting the "stage"--designing an environment and activities that support the learning process. The facilitator/teacher also needs the skill to guide reflection of the learning in order to maximize understanding, which will enable application of the lessons.

The Appreciative Facilitator: Security & Safety
Establishing a safe setting is the responsibility of the appreciative facilitator. If physical activities are part of the learning process, it means making certain that appropriate safety procedures are followed, that participants have a clear understanding of those procedures, and that they know you will be doing all you can to make certain they are physically safe. This includes making certain that activities are mechanically safe, the environment is safe, and that support strategies (such as spotting) are taught and utilized.

Emotional safety is vital for the brain to be open and receptive for learning. The appreciative facilitator builds rapport and trust with others creating an atmosphere of safety. The appreciative perspective helps to create this safe environment. Recall that the appreciative facilitator believes in others, sees them as capable, looks for success, and crafts questions that help others focus on their successes and when they are at their best. Such an environment supports trust and a sense of emotional safety, which allows the brain and heart to open to their fullest capacity for learning.

To see the power in this for yourself, recall a learning experience where your teacher or supervisor/manager taught by criticizing, finding fault, pointing out mistakes, and demanding that you correct your weaknesses. As you immerse yourself in that memory, really go into the thoughts and feelings. How open were you to trying new things for this person? How easy was it to risk putting something out that wasn't perfect? How sure were you that you could actually do it right? How easy was it to focus and learn?

Now recall a learning experience where your teacher or supervisor/manager taught by commenting on the things you did well, on pointing out your strengths, and by encouraging you to attempt even more. He or she may have given you suggestions for future improvements or encouraged you to go for more.

How open were you to trying new things for this person? How easy was it to risk doing something you'd never tried before? How sure were you that you could do more than you thought you could? How easy was it to focus and learn?

The latter is an appreciative facilitator. Individuals working with such facilitators will learn more, be more creative and innovative, stretch further, and find more joy in their learning process.

Low Ropes Challenge Courses
Once the environment has been established, then participants are free to become involved in the learning activities that are designed to enhance the desired understanding, growth, and development. A ropes course—and other experiential learning modalities—are designed to create innovative learning opportunities for developing personal interactive skills and core competencies. These activities can be completed in a short amount of time, and in fact allow people to learn complex concepts many times faster than in a traditional classroom setting. Combining carefully designed activities with appreciative facilitation supports rapid, high impact learning.

The experiential learning process begins with a challenge to participants. Moving through the challenge results in participants experiencing using core competencies and personal abilities that are required to successfully complete the challenge. Skilled appreciative debriefing enables them to become aware of what they experienced, and how to transfer what they experienced to their lives (work, home, relationships, life in general). A key is to ask questions so that the participants do the talking because learning is complete only when individuals have had the opportunity to express their understanding [C. Hannaford].

Traditionally, a low ropes course is an outdoor adventure. It is just one component of a series of adventure-based learning tools, which include such activities as high ropes courses, climbing, white water rafting, sailing, fly fishing, orienteering, and trekking. These adventures are all designed to provide metaphorical environments that bring out inherent skills and abilities that are relevant to the workplace, school setting, and to our lives. Concepts such as leadership, innovative thinking, teamwork, communication, risk-taking, planning, conflict management, multiple intelligence/emotional intelligence, and many others are learned through these activities.

As more and more people are discovering the powerful learning that is accomplished in a short amount of time with ropes courses, the demand for these activities increases. This demand has created the need for portable elements. Portability allows the activities to be brought to the people rather than the other way around, and it solves the challenges of inclement weather. Such flexibility enables greater numbers of people to use these valuable tools and keeps the cost of such use to a minimum. In addition, portability enables training and development programs and educational institutions to integrate these activities into classroom-type learning environments—creating dynamic and extremely effective programs. *(For information on innovative, high impact portable ropes courses, please see References.)*

The Experiential Learning Model
The experiential learning model is a dynamic, cyclical model; in its simplest form it is a four-step process. Experiential learning is about having an experience, reflecting upon it in order to "get conscious," exploring the learning and the metaphors to see how the new awareness can enhance one's life (work, play, school, family), and then applying the awareness in the next challenge activity (or to work and life).

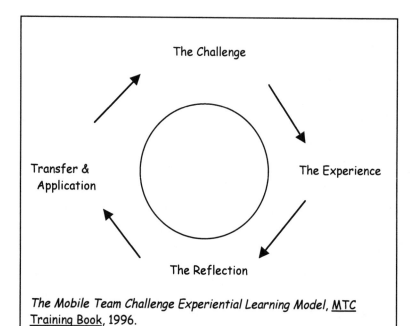

The Challenge

Transfer &
Application

The Experience

The Reflection

The Mobile Team Challenge Experiential Learning Model, <u>MTC</u>
<u>Training Book</u>, 1996.

The Challenge

In a low ropes course, the challenge is the activity
that is presented to the group/participants.   Here the
facilitator presents the activity, typically in the form
of a story. The story engages the imagination,
supports context, encourages a sense of playfulness,
and inspires creativity. Stories involve all the senses,
including imagery, thus improving the chances that
the information will be retained and have meaning
later during the debriefing process. The facilitator's

task during the challenge is to give complete yet succinct instructions, stating only what is necessary information and safety precautions that do not give away solutions. (It is a good idea to remember exactly what you stated so that when asked for clarification, you will be able to repeat exactly the same information.) When questioned, most often the facilitator should simply repeat the instructions. The idea is to be simple and explicit, leaving lots of room for participants to create assumptions. . . or not.

It is here that the facilitator needs to take into account the objectives of the group, the individual and the group needs. This information will inform the decision about what story or metaphor to use to introduce the activity. It will inform the decision as to whether to front-load the activity. (Front-loading is providing added information before the activity that directs the group in some way. In general front-loading should be avoided. Sometimes it is valuable if a group is having difficulty developing as a team. Sometimes it is vital for safety purposes. The appreciative facilitator, believing in the inherent ability of the group, however, would not think to front-load without sufficient evidence that the group needed it or unless it was to further a particular learning objective that could not be achieved otherwise.)

The Experience

The second stage of the Experiential Learning Model is the experience. This is the actual "doing" of the activity; this is where participants work and play resolving the challenge presented. Trial and error, brainstorming, problem-solving, and individual and group dynamics surface. The facilitator's role during this stage is to monitor safety, stay alert for opportunities to re-enforce the learning objectives (introducing handicaps, dropping an appropriate comment), and listen/look for comments and insights that are related to the learning objectives. The appreciative facilitator stays aware of the big picture, but is, of course, looking and listening for what the group is doing well, where they are succeeding, where they are excelling, and where they are practicing the learning objectives well. These will be the focal points for debriefing.

It is perfectly acceptable for the facilitator to take notes during this stage, as long as it does not distract from monitoring safety. If at any time participants suggest actions that might be unsafe, the appreciative facilitator goes on alert but does not take any action in response to a mere suggestion. In keeping with the facilitator's belief in the inherent ability of the group, rather than immediately jumping in, she or he pauses, providing the participants the opportunity to self-manage their safety. If they proceed, however, the facilitator should stop the action for a moment and introduce the safety concern. (This is especially important when a group decides to lift or otherwise physically support one another. Proper lifting, carrying, and body stance are vital for safety of backs, knees, and shoulders.)

Other than these actions, the facilitator is basically not involved during the experience or activity. The group is the focus, the action, and the solution-finder.

The Reflection
The third stage is the reflection; here the group reflects upon the experience and brings to consciousness what they learned and how they worked together. This is where the real skills of the appreciative facilitator are needed. The quality of the reflection and the direction in which it heads will be determined by the questions the facilitator asks. The goal is to carefully craft questions that support the group's awareness of what they did well, especially related to the learning objectives. The more positive the images created during the reflection process, the more positive will be the future actions of the group. Skillful facilitators do very little talking; they simply asks questions.

The facilitator continues to listen and look for metaphors in the conversation—especially as they are related to the environment the participants will return to (school, family, or work). The facilitator can guide a participant toward an insight using a technique called "tailgating." The facilitator leads the debriefing discussion by following (tailgating) the participant's comments with carefully chosen questions that "guide" the participant or the group toward the desired learning outcome. The appreciative facilitator is careful to use this practice when it is appropriate to the learning objectives.

This technique is often used to weave transfer and reflection into a future image that can be anchored in a way that supports its becoming a reality. The appreciative facilitator is careful to ask questions that continuously lead toward desired images and visions, rather than into problems. For example, a participant (Sarah) explains during the debriefing process that she felt that no one would listen to her. The dialogue might continue:

Sarah: No one ever listens to me. When I made a suggestion for how to solve this, no one paid attention. 15 minutes later Peter said it and it was done.

Facilitator: Was anyone aware of Sarah's suggestion?

Participant: I heard her.

Group: We never heard her the
entire time.

Facilitator: And?

Participant: Well, we all just went on.
We got it eventually anyway.

Facilitator: Hmm. Does this ever
happen at work?

Sarah: All the time!!

Facilitator: (To the whole group) Tell me, why did
the group hear Peter? What is it that
those who get heard do to get heard?

Group: We're use to listening to Peter.
They speak up loudly.
They use body language.
They insist on being heard.
They have energy and enthusiasm
behind their idea.

Facilitator: Sarah, do you think any of
these options might work for
you the next time you have
an idea?

Sarah: I can speak more loudly, and I guess I
can insist; though this would be difficult
for me.

Facilitator: What would it sound like if you spoke
up and insisted? What would you be
thinking, feeling, and experiencing that

would support your doing this? Can you give us an example of when you think this might occur at work and what you are going to do?

Sarah: If I spoke up and insisted, I would be feeling a little shy, but when it worked, I would be more apt to do it again. I can imagine the next time we have a staff meeting and I have an idea I might even stand up and say what I have to say.

Facilitator: Are there ways the group could support you?

Sarah: If someone hears me, it would be great to be encouraged.

Facilitator: Group?

Group: We can do that. We can also make sure that everyone has a chance to share his or her ideas. Sarah's not the only one who feels like she doesn't get heard.

Facilitator: So paint a picture for me, group. What will this look and sound like on the next event and back in the work environment? Also tell me what the incredible benefits will be from this decision. . .

Tailgating should be used to follow participant's insights into deeper levels of awareness and learning—targeting positive learning objectives.

The Application/Transfer
The fourth stage is the application or the transfer of the learning to life (school, work, family). The facilitator supports the group in drawing correlations between the activity and their living/working environment. This truly creates the context and connections for rich learning. Though this stage is the fourth step in the process, the skilled facilitator weaves the reflection and application/transfer stages together to enable a seamless transfer of the activity to reality, like the example above. Metaphors, phrases that come from the activity but are great "life" statements, and active images are all-powerful elements to use during this stage. This is where the appreciative facilitator asks the group to create images of what this will look like at school or work. For example, "paint a picture for me of what this planning and follow-through will look like tomorrow in the classroom. Be really specific, who will do what?" Again, the more positive, detailed and powerful the image created, the more positive the future action will be. The facilitator can encourage the group to keep track (perhaps on a flipchart) of the key insights that they are taking from each activity and/or to draw a cartoon or picture of what it would

mean to implement the concepts from this event in their life or workplace. At the end of a series of activities, the group can pull together all of the concepts and create a team statement or draw a team cartoon or image that captures the essence of their learning as it relates to the original desired outcome. Such statements are more effective if they contain bold, dynamic language that creates powerful images, or if their drawings are bold, dramatic images.

It is also appropriate for the facilitator to ask the group how they will utilize what they just learned in the next event; this requires imagining using their newly acquired skills and insights immediately. The appreciative facilitator, knowing that active images lead to future action, encourages the development of positive, detailed and specific images from the group. The facilitator can then look for the implementation of their vision in the next event and acknowledge them for successful implementation.

In experiential learning, the activity truly is the teacher. The value of the lesson, however, is measured by the skill and quality of the appreciative facilitator. Your role as facilitator is a vital component because it is the facilitator who raises the question, focuses on the success, encourages the group to recognize how skillful they are, and helps to create powerful images that truly motivate groups to implement valuable changes in their lives.

Chapter Three

THE ART OF CRAFTING QUESTIONS

Appreciative facilitators are masters of the Socratic method, of using the art of questioning to draw out knowledge and wisdom. They use questions that enable participants to "wake up" and own their knowledge, to recognize their own inherent skills and abilities.

The Key
The key in crafting questions is to know what outcome you are after. This is determined in different ways depending upon what or who you are facilitating. If you are a consultant working with an organization, this will be determined by the outcome your client desires. If you are a teacher, this is determined by your curriculum. If you are a youth counselor, this is determined by the life skills that you seek to teach the children. If you are a therapist, this is determined by the changes your client seeks.

The appreciative facilitator will work to fully understand the desired outcome and/or the dream or vision by talking with the client or students. Often people present outcomes using deficit language. For example, the CEO says, "everyone here needs to stop passing the buck and disowning the problem. No one here is motivated to step up, and we haven't had an innovative suggestion from anyone in years!" The Principal might state, "There is too much noise in the halls, we have kids smoking in the bathrooms, and students are doing poorly on standardized test scores."

The appreciative facilitator, in an effort to be very clear on the desired outcome, invites the client to clarify what _is_ desired, rather than what is not desired. By asking appreciative questions, the appreciative facilitator enables the client to provide an affirmative outcome, a positive vision that will define the goal(s) for the facilitator. For example, the appreciative facilitator might ask the CEO, "Imagine you woke up tomorrow and things at work were just the way you thought they should be, what would it look like? What kind of ownership would people take? How would you know that people were motivated? How could you recognize innovation was occurring? What would be happening that made you think/feel that everyone was in alignment with the mission and vision?" The appreciative facilitator might ask the Principal, "What would you like to see regarding student achievement and student pride in their school, in the broadest sense?"

The appreciative facilitator listens carefully to the individual(s) with whom they will be working. They craft the questions at this initial stage always with an eye towards developing an image or vision of the positive outcome the client desires.

Developing the Program
Based upon the desired outcome, the program is developed by the facilitator. If you are designing a ropes course program, you would make sure to select events that will focus on the skills or concepts that will lead toward the desired outcome. You would sequence these events for safety, skill development, and progressive learning and application. This means you begin with less complex activities, and increase the challenge with each subsequent event. In this way, participants gain greater and greater skill and competence in the desired area, managing more complex and challenging events while implementing and utilizing the desired skills and concepts. Since reflection and application/transfer are key components of effective learning, make sure to leave sufficient time after each event for debriefing and discussion.

Crafting the Questions
Crafting the questions follows directly from having a clearly defined desired outcome. All questions should lead in that direction; they should result in

images that support the desired outcome. When you first begin to practice this, it may seem overly simplified and awkward. As your appreciative perspective develops, however, your questions will dig deeper and be more complex while still being appreciative in nature.

Early on, an easy technique for determining whether the question is appreciative is to see if it leads towards a positive image of the outcome you are after. If the answer is yes, ask it. If the answer is no, reframe it (it is probably a good point; it just needs tweaking). For example, you are facilitating a session for teachers and the desired outcome is effective communication with students. You want to ask, "Why are we not talking with our students like you just did in that event?" STOP. What image(s) will come of this question? It will re-enforce all the images associated with not communicating well. You don't want to ask this question, but the idea to explore this area is a good one. Let's reframe it.

The original idea was to uncover the obstacles or assumptions that keep them from communicating; the appreciative idea is to identify the elements or aspects of their relationship that enable them to communicate well. Same issue, other side of the coin. So, you might ask, "What are some of the important aspects of your relationship that enabled you to communicate the way you did, and how can you develop those same aspects with your students?" What images result from this question? The images will be related to positive aspects of relationships that contribute to communication and ways they might develop those in their student relationships. These images move them closer to the desired outcome.

Opening Questions
Here are some examples of questions that can be asked after an event or adventure. In the first case, the desired outcome is improved communication skills. An activity is selected that requires good listening and communication. After the activity, the opening question might be any of the following:

♦ How did your communication support your success?

♦ What forms of communication were effective and essential to the success of this event?

♦ How important was listening during this event, and what role did it play in your success?

In the next case, the desired outcome is improved leadership skills. An activity is selected that focuses on leadership. Here are some examples of opening questions:

♦ What leadership characteristics were essential to the safety and success of this event?

♦ How did leadership play a role in this event and what important skills surfaced within your team?

♦ Who were your leaders and how did you decide to follow them? What factors were important for you in your decision to follow?

Follow-up questions to these will depend upon the answers that participants give. Remember, you are after details, bold images, and specific instances that will give participants a very clear picture of exactly what good communication or good leadership looks like.

Redirects

If participants point out mistakes, poor leadership, or poor communication skills, craft questions that redirect them towards the desired outcome. Acknowledge their insight and concern, and then head them into the future where it can work well by asking them an appreciative question which tailgates their insight.

Here are a few examples.

♦ *Insight* "There were too many people trying to lead at once, no one was listening, it was a mess." *Redirect* "Great insight. What happened that changed all of that. (if something did). ~or~ "So what needs to happen in this kind of situation?"

♦ *Insight* "I was really uncomfortable following but I didn't feel like I had a choice. I wouldn't have done it if the group hadn't made me."
Redirect "What is important for you in this situation to be comfortable following? What else needs to happen for you so that you choose to participate freely? How can we all feel more comfortable letting others know what we need?"

Transfer and Application

Crafting the transfer and application questions is really about asking the group to get very specific about what these skills and concepts will look like when implemented in life settings. If you have a very clear understanding of a client's environment, then it is easier for you to lead a group into getting very detailed about the imagery. The more detailed the imagery, the bolder the words and visions, the more complete the picture, the greater the chance the group will actually move into it.

For example, a group is working on managing a very chaotic program opening. Every year this opening day creates excess stress that carries over into the program, and no one looks forward to this day with any sense of positive anticipation. You do an activity that involves creating order out of total chaos. During the debriefing process, appreciative questions have the group focusing on all the things they did well that created order. You bring their awareness to the different kinesthetic feelings during chaos and during order. When you shift to transfer, you ask, "Just suppose you've planned your opening day to run as smoothly as this last round of the event, and that you move through the day without much stress. In fact, imagine coming to the end of the day in utter amazement. How did it happen? What will you have done? " Have them get very specific, planning out all the details just as they did with the event, being clear, precise, and careful. Get them to name all the specific activities that must be managed or juggled during the opening and what each of them will do in order to achieve this same level of order and flow so there is a sense of celebration at the end of the day, just as they did during the event.

You can further intensify the imagery by asking them to reflect internally as they each imagine this day, getting them to kinesthetically feel the day without chaos. You might invite them to create a picture, logo, poem, or quote that captures the essence of their plan. This image then can serve as an anchor for their plan and the sense of order.

Then check back with them and see how their opening day went!

Subtlety
Early on it may be beneficial to write out your questions and look at them. Language can be very subtle, and you may not see the direction a question takes you until you see it written out. If you co-facilitate, jot down one another's questions during debriefing so you can review them after your sessions. If they need tweaking, play with different ways of saying the same thing but from the appreciative perspective. The bottom line is always, "Does this question lead toward the desired positive outcome?"

Classroom Settings
The power of the question is very much alive and well in classroom settings, even in traditional settings where students sit behind desks and teachers ask questions and provide feedback for students. Asking appreciative questions that will point the student in the direction you want them to go is the most productive approach. Stating rules and providing structure in pro-active, positive format (telling them what you want them to do rather than what you do not want them to do, giving them approval for desired behavior instead of admonitions) will be more effective. Giving feedback on papers about what they did well, how many they got right (along with what needs correcting, if necessary), will go a long ways towards developing skills and knowledge.

Chapter Four

APPRECIATIVE INQUIRY

There is an Appreciative Inquiry process, which was originally designed by David Cooperrider to be used for organizational development. Some of you may be interested in weaving the Appreciative Inquiry process into an experiential learning program, and the following information will be helpful for you.

What is Appreciative Inquiry?
Appreciative Inquiry (AI) is an approach, a methodology, a way of perceiving and interacting that transforms the way we experience human systems and organizations. Basically, it is an approach that seeks to discover what gives life to organizations and individuals, to uncover the positive core that is working when a person or group is at its best. AI is grounded in extensive research across diverse fields (from medicine to education to cultural anthropology). This research underscores the concept that what we believe in and focus on determines our outcome and how we reach it. AI proposes we focus on assets and positive, desired outcomes in order to facilitate change and success.

The AI process can be used to identify when individuals and organizations are at their best, identify assets, and engage in the process of dreaming—where does the group want to go. Instead of "needs and problems," individuals and organizations identify personal capabilities and the organization's "positive core". They also develop profound future visions for the organization based upon this positive core, a means for achieving that vision, and the enthusiasm and motivation to bring it into reality.

In applying the AI process, the initial step is the *Definition*, where the guiding principles are identified; here we clarify goals or the desired outcome. AI then proposes four additional steps toward achieving the desired outcome:

1. *Discovery*, where stories of past successes are shared in a carefully designed interview process;
2. *Dream*, where visions of the ideal future are imagined and shared;
3. *Design*, where bold statements are developed that support movement toward the dream based upon the positive core identified during Discovery; and
4. *Destiny/Delivery*, where actual steps are taken toward making the dream reality.

Ultimately these are the same goals a facilitator has for a group. A facilitator starts with the definition or guiding inspiration—what outcome does the group desire? The ultimate goal of the facilitator is to

◆ enable the group to develop an awareness of their inherent skills and abilities,

◆ to learn new and valuable skills and insights,

◆ to recognize how things "could work in the best of all possible worlds," and

◆ to design a plan for how to actually make it happen.

The experiential facilitator does this through activities designed specifically to draw out the desired skills and abilities within the context of "working" on challenges. Appreciative debriefing will lead the group through the four AI phases:

1. **Discovery** *How did you succeed at this event? What group skills did you use? When was the group at its best? What did you value about one another in this process? What did you value about yourself?*

2. **Dream** *Imagine you return to work and overnight something incredible has occurred. When you arrive at work, you know that everything that was learned today will be continued in the workplace. As you look around, interact, and begin work you are convinced this is the case. What changes do you see/hear/feel that enable you to conclude this? What is different about the people? About you? About the*

atmosphere? About interactions? What role do you play in bringing this about?

3. **Design** *Specifically, what have you learned from this activity that will support the vision just described? What does everyone have to agree to and commit to? What specifically will you do?*

4. **Destiny/Delivery** *Well, you will have the chance to carry out that design in the next event. It will be a great opportunity to practice and to see if there are additional concepts or skills you will want to add.*

There is a perfect fit between the AI Process and the Experiential Learning model. The goals are similar, the phases of AI match the phases of the Experiential Learning Model, and the AI principles (below) are a perfect guide for the Appreciative Facilitator's practice:

➤ **The way we know is fateful.** Groups will become aware, understand and know what they did on activities by the questions that are asked. The way they understand what they experienced is fateful; it will effect their future actions. Therefore, appreciative facilitators take to heart the importance of their language, attitude, style, and focus of attention.

➤ **Change begins the moment you ask the first question.** The group will move in the direction the facilitator directs. Appreciative facilitators craft their questions carefully in order to support positive change for the group.

➢ **We are open books**. There is no absolute about the way a person, an organization or a group is. It all depends upon your focus and attention. Appreciative facilitators choose to look for and focus on the group at its best, where they are successful, and where they are developing and changing in relation to the desired outcome.

➢ **Deep change results from active images of the future**. Questions and language create images for listeners; change results when images of the future are active. Since facilitators ask lots of questions, appreciative facilitators pay attention to the questions they ask. They find ways to help groups develop strong, active future images of how they will apply the lessons they have learned. In addition to discussion, they may use poetry, journaling, sculpting, drawing, or photography.

➢ **The more positive the question, the greater and longer lasting the change**. Appreciative facilitators craft unconditionally positive questions, making sure that all aspects of their communication convey the question in unconditionally positive terms (body language, verbiage, tone, etc.).

Chapter Five

THE PROMISE

Becoming an appreciative facilitator is truly about seeing the world through very different lenses and recognizing the powerful person that you are. It means:

♦ Realizing the effects your beliefs have on others, and taking responsibility for those beliefs.

♦ Changing those beliefs that are not congruent with who you are and how you want to effect the world around you.

♦ Realizing the effects your focus of attention and thought patterns have on your perceptions, reactions, and behavior and taking responsibility for being in charge of your focus and thoughts.

♦ Choosing to be fully responsible for the language (verbal and nonverbal) that you use, carefully choosing language that supports desired outcomes.

♦ Acknowledging and accepting the "power of your position" as a facilitator/teacher, wielding that power responsibly and effectively.

♦ Allowing yourself to shift your world paradigm without the harsh judgement and criticism from some "inner voice".

♦ Recognizing the importance of context, experience, and security/safety in the overall learning environment and making certain that your teaching and facilitating are congruent with effective learning.

Committing to become an appreciative facilitator means a commitment to change your life. It is not likely that it will come overnight, but with patience, support from colleagues, and your resolve, it will happen. The promise is that like your clients and students, you too will hold positive active images of the future for yourself and for others. Your world will become one filled with joy, beauty, hope, creativity, and the sparkle of personal motivation. . . and this can't help but have a positive effect on you!

Appendix I

POSITIVE IMAGE→POSITIVE ACTION

[Based upon **"Positive Image, Positive Action of Organizing**," David L. Cooperrider].

There are six areas of research, which support the appreciative approach:
The Placebo Effect comes out of medical research documenting that the belief the patient has in the doctor and the prescribed medicine are what cures the disease. With consistency, inert pills cure diverse diseases in double-blind studies. Medical research also documents that the belief that a patient has, the images she or he carries—about the doctor, the disease, the cure, or the cause—play a significant role in their recovery. Bottom line: believing the best will occur actually helps bring it about. [Beecher, 1955; Thite, Tursky, and Schwartz, 1985; Ornstein and Sobel, 1987; Human Options, Norman Cousins, 1981; White, Tursky, and Schwartz, 1985; Jaffe & Bresler, 1980; O'Regan, 1983.]

The Pygmalion Effect comes out of research in education. Research done with elementary school children shows that the belief the teacher held about the child compelled the child to behave according to the teacher's beliefs. The teacher's belief about the child's abilities resulted in teacher behavior that led the child to behave exactly as the teacher expected. Bottom line: as the teacher/parent/boss (facilitator) believes, so the student/child/worker (participant) becomes. [Uussim, 1986; Rosenthal and Rubin, 1978; Parsons et al, 1982; King, 1971; Cooper and Good, 1983; Brophy and Good, 1974; Crano and Mellon, 1978; Humphreys and Stubbs, 1977; Eden and Shani, 1982; Deaux and Emswiller, 1974; Hastie and Kumar, 1979; Darley and Gross, 1983; Rist, 1970; Rubovitz and Maehr, 1973; Weinstein, 1976; Cooper, 1979; Brohpy and Good, 1974; Swann and Snyder, 1980; Jussim, 1986; Brophy and Good, 1974.]

Positive Effect and Affect comes out of research in psychology and medicine. Change happens the moment the question is asked, the moment the statement is made. The effect is a whole-person effect—body, mind and spirit are impacted. This can be demonstrated by asking for a volunteer. Ask the person to hold their arm out to the side and resist as you press down upon it. You will both get a reading regarding their strength. Ask them to lower the arm. Now have them recall a time in the recent past where they were ashamed, embarrassed, or otherwise felt bad about their actions. (They are not to share this). Then ask them to raise their arm again and resist. This time, you will both notice a significant drop in ability. They will be awestruck. Try again. Even a third time. With their arm lowered, ask them to now think of the last time they did or said something they were so proud of, where people around them gave them accolades and praise. When they have the image, ask them to hold their arm out and resist. You will both notice their strength has returned. Often it will be even stronger than the first time. [The bigger and stronger the person, the greater the difference in strength!] Bottom line: The questions you ask, the language you use impacts the people around you—supporting (or not) their ability to act and move forward. [Sheikh and Panagiotou, 1975; Watson and Clark, 1984; Seligman, 1975; Brewin, 1985; Peterson and Seligman, 1984; Beck, 1967; Schultz, 1984; Ley and Freeman, 1984.]

Imbalanced Inner Dialogue comes out of research in the field of psychology. The language and images that are created by inner dialogue effects the overall health and vitality of a person or an organization. The research indicates that one needs at least two positive images for every negative to create a positive residual effect. This goes for dialogues in the hallways, around water coolers, in our homes, in student parking lots, and inside our heads. (Incidentally, the research also shows that in relationships, there needs to be a 5 to 1 ratio—positive to negative). Bottom line: Monitor your self-talk and your dialogues, make sure there is more emphasis on the positive. [Cooperrider.]

The Rise and Fall of Cultures even shows a distinct pattern around positive and negative. Cultural anthropology has documented that cultures where people believe they have some ability to effect the future, where they come together in groups to discuss ideas and everyone's voice is valued, where art, music, and theatre are valued are cultures that are rising. These cultures are alive, developing, growing, and evolving. When these aspects of the culture diminish, the culture declines. If these aspects disappear, the culture will also collapse. This applies to civilizations as well as small sub-cultures. Bottom line: empowered individuals who are encouraged to participate, co-create, and innovate help keep an organization alive and thriving. [Cooperrider]

Affirmative Capability simply means that the mind can only wrap itself around a positive image. What does your mind envision when it hears, "Don't think of a red car!"? Imagine what has been happening with campaigns for "Don't do drugs!" and "Don't smoke!" There have been many studies, most of them around athletics regarding affirmative capability. [Cooperrider]

Appendix II

EXPERIENTIAL LEARNING MODEL: WHAT THE FACILITATOR DOES

The Challenge
This is an event that a group will be challenged to do.
♦ The *facilitator's role*:
1. Choose the event.
2. Set up the event (or supervise the set-up).
3. Explain the challenge--simply, succinctly without giving clues or suggestions, unless you intend to front-load.
4. Underscore safety concerns (in a timely way, without disclosing solutions).

The Experience
The group does the event.
♦ The *facilitator's role:*
1. Monitor the big picture.
2. Monitor for safety.
3. Observe, take notes.
4. Look for special learning opportunities; e.g., times when blindfolding someone will support the learning outcomes.

Reflection
The group reflects on the experience.

♦ The *facilitator's role*:
1. Ask appreciative questions.
2. Share observations and ask questions based upon observations.
3. Monitor group process, see the big picture.
4. Tailgate appropriately to underscore desired outcomes.
5. Look for the links, metaphors and ways to weave the learning into application/transfer.

Application & Transfer
The group explores ways to use what they have learned.

♦ The *facilitator's role*:
1. Support the transfer of learning by asking carefully crafted questions and weaving reflection into application/transfer.
2. Share relevant models that will aid in the transfer of learning.
3. Use journaling to support the transfer.
4. Provide ample opportunity for discussion, planning, and developing "real world" actions to be taken.

Appendix III

PLANNING FOR AN EXPERIENTIAL LEARNING PROGRAM (SUCH AS A ROPES COURSE)

The following is a general outline to help facilitators plan for an experiential activity or a series of activities, such as a ropes course.

Days before the Event(s)

A. Define the desired outcome and your objectives. If you have the Mobile Team Challenge Facilitator Manual, you can use the Goal Reference Matrix to help you. Other books sometimes have activities cross-referenced with learning concepts to help make planning easier.

B. Select activities that will support your desired outcome and sequence them for success; maximize the incremental and applied learning.

C. Make sure the course or equipment that you want to use will be available at the time you need it (reserve it, if necessary).

D. Know your participants, including any special needs, medical concerns, or emotional challenges.

E. Plan according to your goals and the desired outcome, the groups' ability, the time you have available, and the location.

F. Decide upon a story or metaphorical setting for the event(s).

G. Know if you need to front-load and have a plan for how you will do that.

H. Review safety procedures and precautions.

The Day

A. Check in with your co-facilitator, if appropriate.

B. Check your equipment or the event(s) to make sure that everything is safe and you have what you need.

C. Make sure you have first aid equipment.

D. Have participants complete Release Agreement and medical forms, if appropriate.

E. Provide safety instruction and training for the group.

F. Describe the activity/challenge.

G. Monitor safety during the activity.

H. Facilitate the debriefing process: reflection and application

I. Go on to the next event, if you are doing a series.

Closure

A. Ask participants to complete evaluation forms.

B. Return equipment or secure the area.

C. Debrief with co-facilitator or personally reflect on your session. What went well? When were you at your best? What did you value most? How will it be even better next time?

Appendix IV

GENERAL SAFETY OUTLINE

This book is not a stand-alone training book for those interested in offering experiential learning programs. The author recommends you attend formal training in order to make sure you receive all the information needed to offer a safe and educationally sound program. (If you are interested in a formal training in appreciative facilitation for a ropes course, you can contact Mobile Team Challenge.) This section is a brief overview of safety; it should not be considered complete.

Typically, experiential learning activities are "challenge by choice" meaning no one is ever forced to participate. Challenge by choice is generally introduced in conjunction with three "learning zones":

♦ **The Comfort Zone,** where one is typically on "cruise control." Learning is at a minimum here because the brain is easily preoccupied with other topics.

♦ **The Stretch Zone**, where one is still comfortable, but is also being personally, emotionally or physically stretched. Learning is at a maximum here because the person is alert and attention is focused on the task at hand.

♦ **The Panic Zone**, where one is way beyond comfort, the primary concern is survival. Learning shrinks to zero here because the person seeks only to protect and defend themselves.

To maximize learning and safety, you want people to step into the stretch zone; how far they step is their choice. If part of an activity brings them too close to panic for comfort, offer them another way to be involved.

As an experiential learning facilitator, your primary responsibility is safety. As a facilitator you should:
♦ Have current first aid/CPR as a minimum medical certification.
♦ Plan ahead.
♦ Know that safety is your primary responsibility.
♦ Check-in with your co-facilitator.
♦ Pay attention and use your best judgement.
♦ Stay aware of the big picture.
♦ Monitor the equipment and the action.
♦ Look for learning opportunities, "transfer" moments.
♦ Know the equipment, activities, and the group.
♦ Use appreciative facilitation skills and have the appropriate skills and knowledge to guide the group with whom you are working.

The following are the safety concerns related to the group with whom you will be working:

Know the abilities of the group and any medical or emotional conditions that are of concern.

Know the group's goals or desired outcome.

Use "handicaps" (like blindfolding someone) only when they will support the desired learning and not if they will create a safety concern.

Know the participant:facilitator ratio standard for the activities you will be doing and do not exceed that ratio (for example, 15:1 for most low ropes course activities).

Know the desired outcome and select and sequence events to achieve that outcome safely.

Involve participants with their safety and the safety of the group. Make sure participants understand safety procedures and acknowledge their willingness to be responsible for their own and the group's safety.

♦ Stay alert for "red flags" (physical, emotional, or behavioral danger signals).

Make sure participants are dressed appropriately for the activity and for the location; jewelry and personal items that might cause injury should be removed.

As a facilitator, you will also need to make sure the environment is safe:

♦ Make sure the area is free and clear of danger (rocks, branches, desks, chairs, sharp corners).

♦ Weather conditions should be safe: not outdoors in electric storms, sunscreen, water, and hats for hot weather outdoors.

♦ If you are using portable equipment, the ground should be relatively flat.

♦ Create an emotionally safe environment by practicing appreciative facilitation.

♦ If you have to move equipment, make sure it is handled safety, spotted, and lifted appropriately.

Make sure to cover all the administrative bases as well:

♦ Know and practice all safety procedures from the manual that accompanies the activity or equipment that you are using.

♦ Complete a written record of your safety procedures after each session so that you have a record that indicates you covered safety.

♦ Complete an incident report form if you have an accident.

♦ Review medical forms for red flags or concerns; talk with any participant that is of concern.

Appendix V

RESOURCES

Rather than listing extensive resources for Appreciative Inquiry, Experiential Learning, and Brain-Based Learning this reference section will provide you with enough information to head you towards locations that have extensive resource lists.

APPRECIATIVE INQUIRY RESOURCES/REFERENCES

Cooperrider, Sorense, Whitney, and Jaegar, Rethinking Human Organization Toward a Positive Theory of Change, Stipes Publishing, 1999.

Cooperrider, David, "Positive Image, Positive Action of Organizing."

Hammond, Sue Annis, The Thin Book, Thin Book Publishing, 1998. (Available at www.thinbook.com)

Srivastva and Cooperrider, Appreciative Management and Leadership: The Power of Positive Thought and Action in Organization, Lakeshore Communications, 1999.

Watkins, Jane Magruder and Bernard J. Mohr, Appreciative Inquiry: Change at the Speed of Imagination, Jossey-Bass, Inc., 2001.

AI listserv: The AI discussion list is hosted by the David Eccles School of Business at the University of Utah. Jack Brittain is the list administrator. For subscription information, go to:
http://lists.business.utah.edu/mailman/listinfo/ailist

EXPERIENTIAL LEARNING

Mobile Team Challenge: providers of the most innovative, high performance portable low ropes course as well as facilitator training. Cheri Torres is co-founder, along with Carolyn Rainey Morton, of Mobile Team Challenge.
3247 E. Lamar Alexander Parkway
Maryville, TN 37804
Phone 865-681-0146 Fax 865-982-7721
www.mobileteamchallenge.com

The Association for Experiential Education
An international organization for experiential education facilitators. Special groups include Experienced-based Training and Development, Schools & Universities, and Adventures Therapy.
2305 Canyon Boulevard, Suite 100
Boulder, CO 80302
Phone 303-440-8844 Fax 303-440-9581
www.aee.org

Experiential Learning Activity Books
Cain, Jim and Barry Jolliff, Teamwork/ Teamplay, Kendall/Hunt Publishing, IA, 1998.

Priest, Simon & Karl Rohnke, <u>101 of the best Corporate Teambuilding Activities We Know!</u>, Learning Unlimited Corporation, OK, 2000.

Rohnke, Karl, <u>Quicksilver</u>, Kendall/Hunt Publishing, IA, 1995.

Sikes, Sam, <u>Executive Marbles</u>, Learning Unlimited Corporation, OK, 1998.

Sikes, Sam, <u>Feeding the Zircon Gorilla,</u> Learning Unlimited Corporation, OK, 1995.

Learning Unlimited Publishers
888-622-4203

Kendall Hunt Publishers
800-228-0810

Experiential Learning Tools
Portable low ropes challenge courses, Mobile Team Challenge, 888-681-0146.

TekTrek^{TM}, portable, high tech orienteering course designed by Orion Learning and sold by Mobile Team Challenge, 888-681-0146.

BRAIN-BASED LEARNING

Hannaford, Carla, <u>Smart Moves: Why Learning Is Not All In Your Head</u>, Great Ocean Publishers, VA, 1995.

Hart, Leslie A., <u>Human Brain & Human Learning</u>, Books for Educators, Inc., Washington, 1998.

Healy, Jane M., <u>Endangered Minds</u>, A Touchstone Book, Simon & Schuster, NY, 1990.

Kovalik, Susan, <u>ITI: The Model</u>, Susan Kovalik & Associates Publisher, 1994.

Schlechty, Phillip C., <u>Inventing Better Schools</u>, Jossey-Bass Publishers, San Francisco, 1997.

Randall, Susan, "Brain research applied to teaching," *Casa Grande Dispatch*, Casa Grande, AZ, 2001.

ABOUT THE AUTHOR

Cheri Torres, MBA, MA, left the corporate world to focus on facilitating personal change for others in 1984. Since that time she has worked with corporate groups, community organizations and schools to support people interested in developing their own potential and that of their organization. Experiential training and development has been her primary focus. In 1996, she saw the need and opportunity to bring portable ropes courses and training to a world that was discovering the power of experiential learning. She teamed up with co-founder Carolyn Rainey Morton, and they designed Mobile Team Challenge, the most innovative, high performance portable low ropes course, which won the Creativity Award from the Association for Experiential Education. In 1999, Cheri integrated Appreciative Inquiry into the MTC facilitator training, making it the first Appreciative Facilitator training course in the country. Mobile Team Challenge has trained hundreds of teachers, counselors, trainers, and facilitators in the practice of Appreciative Facilitation.